My Community

By

Grace Jones

Crabtree Publishing Company
www.crabtreebooks.com
1-800-387-7650

Published in Canada
Crabtree Publishing
616 Welland Avenue
St. Catharines, ON
L2M 5V6

Published in the United States
Crabtree Publishing
PMB 59051
350 Fifth Ave, 59th Floor
New York, NY 10118

Published by Crabtree Publishing Company in 2018

First Published by Book Life in 2017
Copyright © 2017 Book Life

Author: Grace Jones

Editors: Grace Jones, Janine Deschenes

Design: Evie Wright

Proofreader: Petrice Custance

**Production coordinator and
    prepress technician (interior):** Margaret Amy Salter

Prepress technician (covers): Ken Wright

Print coordinator: Margaret Amy Salter

Photographs

iStock: kali9 p 14

All other images from Shutterstock

Printed in the USA/072017/CG20170524

Library and Archives Canada Cataloguing in Publication

Jones, Grace, 1990-, author
        My community / Grace Jones.

(Our values)
Includes index.
Issued in print and electronic formats.
ISBN 978-0-7787-3702-5 (hardcover).--
ISBN 978-0-7787-3875-6 (softcover).--
ISBN 978-1-4271-1984-1 (HTML)

        1. Communities--Juvenile literature. 2. Community life--Juvenile literature. 3. Social participation--Juvenile literature. I. Title.

HM756.J66 2017   j307   C2017-902503-1
                                                                      C2017-902504-X

Library of Congress Cataloging-in-Publication Data

Names: Jones, Grace, 1990- author.
Title: My community / Grace Jones.
Description: New York : Crabtree Publishing Company, [2017] |
    Series: Our values | Audience: Age: 5-8. | Audience: K to Grade 3. |
    Includes index.
Identifiers: LCCN 2017016730 (print) | LCCN 2017020459 (ebook) |
    ISBN 9781427119841 (Electronic HTML) |
    ISBN 9780778737025 (reinforced library binding) |
    ISBN 9780778738756 (pbk.)
Subjects: LCSH: Communities--Juvenile literature.
Classification: LCC HM756 (ebook) | LCC HM756 .J6376 2017 (print) |
    DDC 307--dc23
LC record available at https://lccn.loc.gov/2017016730

Contents

Words that look like **this** can be found in the glossary on page 24.

What Is a Community?

A community is a group of people that live, work, and play in the same area.

4

Communities are found all over the world. Every community is different. People can be part of many different communities at the same time.

Different Communities

Some communities are very small, such as the community in a neighborhood. Other communities are very big. Whole countries can be communities.

Some communities live in villages. Other communities live in cities.

Why Are Communities Important?

Living in a community makes it easy to make friends and work with others. We can learn about others and celebrate the things that make us the same and different.

Communities can also help you feel like you **belong**.

Different Cultures

People from different **cultures** often live in the same community. Learning about the different cultures in our communities helps us see how we are all **unique**.

Communities often celebrate the different cultures that they include with events such as parades.

People Who Help You

People in a community work together. They help and care for each other. Every person helps make their community a better place to live.

Some people in a community have special jobs that help keep the community safe.

Police Officer

Doctor

Firefighter

13

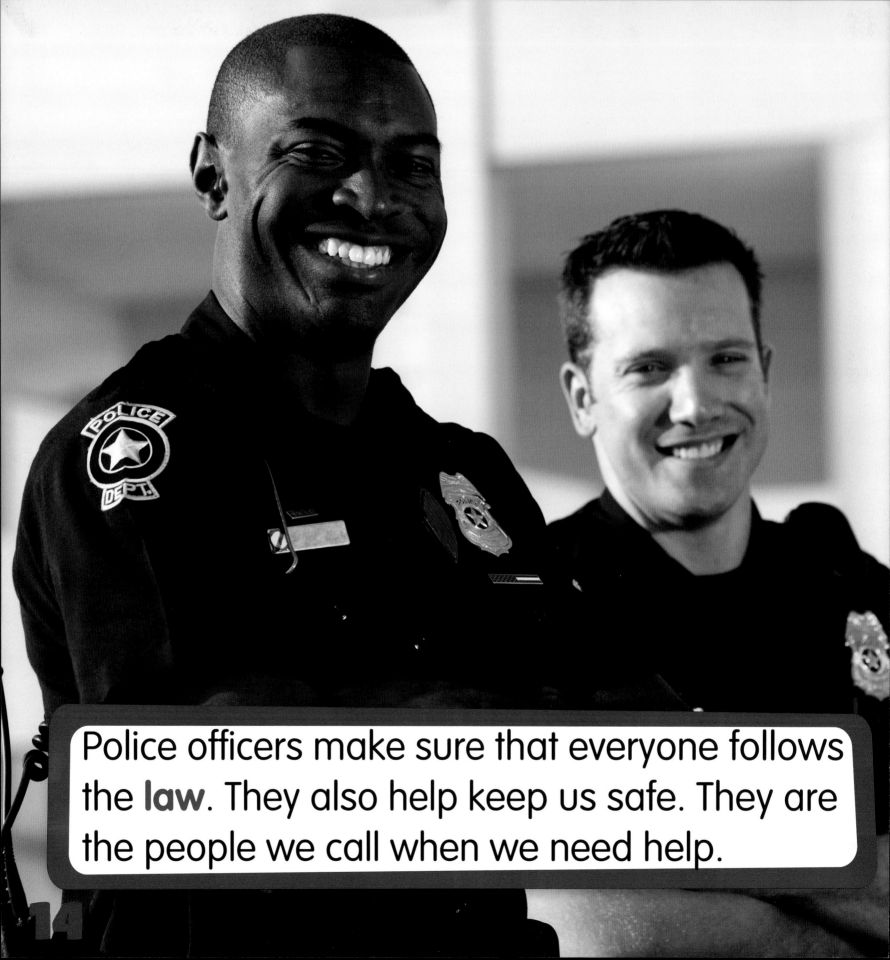

Police officers make sure that everyone follows the **law**. They also help keep us safe. They are the people we call when we need help.

Firefighters help people who are in danger from fires. They also put out fires.

Doctors are people who look after you when you are sick. They help keep their communities healthy.

16

Teachers help you learn how to read and write. They also teach us how to treat others with **respect**.

At School

Every school is a community. A school community includes your classmates, teachers, and anyone else at school such as volunteers, janitors, and your principal.

You can make your school community a good place to learn by being kind to your classmates, listening to your teacher, and respecting others.

At Home

The people in your family are often part of the same communities that you are, such as your neighborhood community or culture.

Your family can help teach you about the communities you are part of.

Global Community

Even though people belong to many different communities…

...we all also belong to one big global community! We all share Earth, the planet where we live.

Glossary

belong   To feel like you are a part of something

cultures   The beliefs and behaviors of a group of people

law   The rules that we all must follow

respect   A feeling that someone or something is good and important

unique   The only one; not like anyone or anything else

Index